SELF TALK
BUT
YOU CAN EAVESOROP TOO

* QUOTES TO LOVE BY *

DOMINIQUE JONES

"No matter what relationship we don't have, we'll always have one with God"
-Dōmo said it

"Praying for an easy life is not the goal, it's praying for strength to endure the difficult one"
-Dōmo said it

#Selftalk

"Don't let your condition hinder your position"
-Dōmo said it

"Happiness is an inside job"
-Dōmo said it

#Selftalk

"Don't dial down your victory...a "W" IS A "W" no matter the contrary"
—Dōmo said it

"Don't let the only time you help someone is when you're good because someone helped you when they weren't"
—Dōmo said it

#Selftalk

"The same ppl that said you can't and you won't are scared that you will be"
—Dōmo said it

"You don't have to root for me but at least respect my progress"
—Dōmo said it

#Selftalk

"There are ppl that are willing to sacrifice themselves to make sure you're at your best. Don't overlook those. You didn't know what that took"
—Dōmo said it

"You should always be in a state of growing"
—Dōmo said it

#Selftalk

"Always remember...someone's effort is a reflection of their interest in you"
-Dōmo said it

"As you grow, don't forget the ones that helped deep root you"
-Dōmo said it

#Selftalk

"Don't wish change so quickly because you may not be able to handle it once you get it"
-Dōmo said it

"Your insecurities causes you to change up...not God"
-Dōmo said it

#Selftalk

SELFTALK

"Stay kind. It makes you beautiful"
-Dōmo said it

"When you feel happy about your future, you prepare even if it looks impossible"
-Dōmo said it

#Selftalk

"Happiness doesn't make you grateful, gratefulness makes you happy"
-Dōmo said it

"Your definition is what you want you say, not what they see"
-Dōmo said it

#Selftalk

"Find your willpower...your future needs you"
—Dōmo said it

"Your energy introduces you before you speak"
—Dōmo said it

#Selftalk

"Don't let your bad days overtake the real you...your pain is a side dish not a main course"
−Dōmo said it

"Self evaluation is key. Check yourself so someone won't take credit for your progress"
−Dōmo said it

#Selftalk

"Live life on purpose...with a purpose"
-Dōmo said it

"Check your posture of heart when someone gets blessed before you"
-Dōmo said it

#Selftalk

"Teach ppl how to handle you, they've never dealt with you before"
-Dōmo said it

"Show patience with others, you're still learning you"
-Dōmo said it

#Selftalk

"Opinions are just that...don't define it as validation"
-Dōmo said it

"Glean to the ones that see past what they see physically"
-Dōmo said it

#Selftalk

"God gave us this life for a reason, remind him why"
-Dōmo said it

"Don't let ppl convince you their way in your situation when they aren't nor have ever been there...they're a support system not an advice counselor"
-Dōmo said it

#Selftalk

#SELFTALK

"Today may be a bad day, but don't overlook the good day you just had"
—Dōmo said it

"You're only limit is your mind"
—Dōmo said it

#Selftalk

"Stop shrinking into places you've outgrown"
-Dōmo said it

"Everyone has their perks. Don't think because theirs looks different yours aren't wanted"
-Dōmo said it

#Selftalk

#SELFTALK

"Promote you...you're somebody's answer"
-Dōmo said it

"Your short term challenges aren't your long term no's"
-Dōmo said it was

#Selftalk

"There's a difference between an injury and a condition...one's a temporary affliction. Don't compare the two"
-Dōmo said it

"Believe in the law on confession....Believe what you speak"
-Dōmo said it

#Selftalk

"The same ppl that said you can't and you won't are scared that you will be"
-Dōmo said it

"I'm glad you're blessed but I'm NEXT"
-Dōmo said it

#Selftalk

#SELFTALK

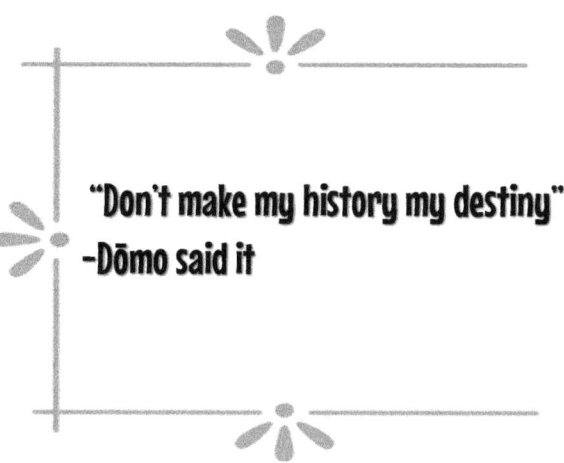

"Don't make my history my destiny"
-Dōmo said it

"Start small and try to make them habits"
Dōmo said it

#Selftalk

"Situations may not ever change but your perspective should"
-Dōmo said it

"Sometimes we suffer because we deny when ppl offer to help us. Even the strongest get weak"
-Dōmo said it

#Selftalk

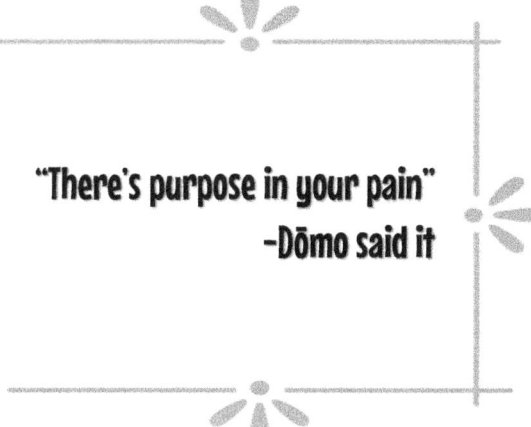

#Selftalk

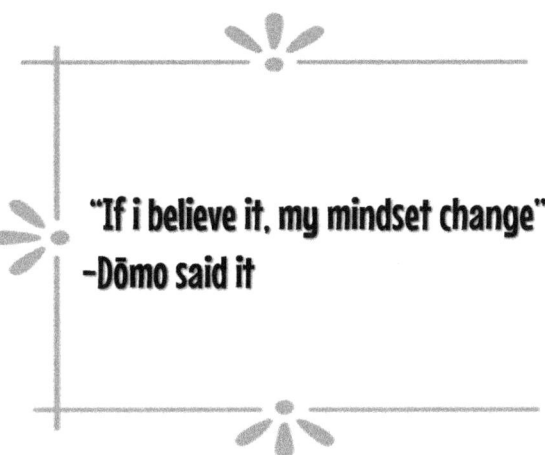

"If i believe it, my mindset change"
-Dōmo said it

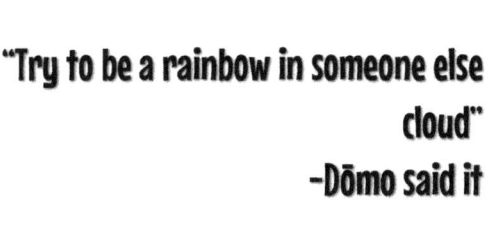

"Try to be a rainbow in someone else cloud"
-Dōmo said it

#Selftalk

"Everything you go through is intentional"
-Dōmo said it

"Ppl are blessed just because you showed up"
-Dōmo said it

#Selftalk

"Your journey will help others heal...remember that when you feel like you're tapped out"
-Dōmo said it

"Not all strength is physical...mental strength is stronger than any muscle you have"
-Dōmo said it

#Selftalk

"Magnify the small victories, not everyone knows how much that took"
-Dōmo said it

"If you're blessed to be different, don't ever change"
-Dōmo said it

#Selftalk

"Start where you are. Use what you have. Do what you can"
-Dōmo said it

"Find your way and rock it with confidence"
-Dōmo said it

#Selftalk

"Remind yourself what you've been able to overcome. You're more powerful than you think"
—Dōmo said it

"Make them stop and stare. You're too authentic to walk past"
—Dōmo said it

#Selftalk

SELFTALK

"Self confidence is the best outfit. Get it in every color"
-Dōmo said it

"Like who you are but love who you're becoming"
-Dōmo said it

… # #Selftalk

"You may have some scars but who doesn't? The only difference is yours are visible"
-Dōmo said it

"I'm not lazy. I'm a warrior. I fight a fight that you'll never understand"
-Dōmo said it

#Selftalk

"Breathe. You've come out of things that you never knew you had the strength for. Don't doubt yourself this time"
-Dōmo said it

"Your last fight made you even stronger for this...and you didn't even realize it"
-Dōmo said it

#Selftalk

"You can't make everything. Don't push yourself just to say "you went""
-Dōmo said it

"People may not understand but when you need to shut down, DO JUST THAT"
-Dōmo said it

#Selftalk

"The power of "no" will save your life...literally"
-Dōmo said it

"Make the best out of your situations...you're in it now"
-Dōmo said it

#Selftalk

"Strength has a new meaning when you have to fight everyday for it"
-Dōmo said it

"Focus on the effort. You really are trying"
-Dōmo said it

#Selftalk

"It's something to see you holding yourself together even when you feel like shattering. It may not look pretty or feel graceful. Don't stop"
-Dōmo said it

"You're battling things your smile will never tell them about"
-Dōmo said it

#Selftalk

"I'm not looking for sympathy. I'm not looking for attention. I'm in pain. I just want relief"
-Dōmo said it

"It's ok if the only thing you do today is breathe"
-Dōmo said it

#Selftalk

"There's no better representation of strength than someone who isn't afraid of being themselves...flaws included"
-Dōmo said it

"The moment you give up physically, your mind gives up mentally"
-Dōmo said it

#Selftalk

"Just because they don't see it, doesn't mean you're not whole"
-Dōmo said it

"Your speed doesn't matter. Forward is forward"
-Dōmo said it

#Selftalk

"My disabilities don't define me...I define my disabilities"
—Dōmo said it

"Live with it. Don't be stuck in it"
—Dōmo said it

#Selftalk

"Being disabled is a condition. Being handicap is a position"
-Dōmo said it

"Pain may always be there but suffering is a choice"
-Dōmo said it

#Selktalk

"How you feel is way more important than how it looks"
—Dōmo said it

"Remind yourself this is just a chapter, not your whole story"
—Dōmo said it

#Selftalk

"One day you will tell your story of how you overcame what you went through and it will be someone's survival guide"
-Dōmo said it

"Strive for progress...perfection is overrated"
-Dōmo said it

#Selftalk

"Sometimes you gotta give yourself a pep talk"
-Dōmo said it

"Don't let ppl only look at the outer condition that they don't recognize the inner appearance"
-Dōmo said it

#Selftalk

"Your future is way more valuable than your temporary situation"
-Dōmo said it

"I am enough. Always have been enough. Always will be enough"
-Dōmo said it

#Selftalk

"If it doesn't get better, you get better"
-Dōmo said it

"Dare to thank God even it doesn't make sense"
-Dōmo said it

#Selftalk

"Ppl know your worth. They just hope you don't"
-Dōmo said it

"If you don't rest your soul in Jesus, you'll never find peace and purpose"
-Dōmo said it

#Selftalk

"Forget all the reasons it didn't work and work on the one reason why it will"
-Dōmo said it

"God is going to use every broken piece to create an original"
-Dōmo said it

#Selftalk

"The goal is to grow so strong on the inside that nothing on the outside can affect your inner self"
-Dōmo said it

"Don't adapt to the situation. Be influenced by the situation"
-Dōmo said it

#Selftalk

"Don't let the disability fool you"...#Damagedbutnotdead...You still have value

- Author with earmuffs

www.ingramcontent.com/pod-product-compliance
Lightning Source LLC
LaVergne TN
LVHW051225070526
838200LV00057B/4610